The Perfect Date:

A 40 **D**ay **D**evotional & **J**ournal

*~ to a new **E**ncounter with God*

COPYRIGHT © Tammy Bradford 2011

ISBN: 978-1-257-09962-7

Cover Design by: Chapter 3 by Design

ALL RIGHTS RESERVED. All rights reserved. No part of this publication may be reproduced or utilized in any form or by any means, electronic or mechanical, including photocopying and microfilm, without permission in writing from the publisher or author.

Unless otherwise indicated, all Scripture quotations are taken from the *King James Version* (KJV) of the Bible. Scripture taken from *THE MESSAGE* copyright (c) by Eugene H. Peterson, 1993, 1994, 1995. Used by permission of NavPress Publishing Group. Scripture quotations taken from *The Amplified Bible* are taken *from THE AMPLIFIED BIBLE, EXPANDED EDITION* Copyright (c) 1987 by the Zondervan Corporation and the Lockman Foundation. All rights reserved. Scripture quotations marked *NKJV* are taken from *The New King James Version* Copyright (c) 1982 by Thomas Nelson, Inc. Scripture quotations marked *NIV* are taken from the *HOLY BIBLE, NEW INTERNATIONAL VERSION* Copyright (c) 1973, 1978, 1984, International Bible Society. Used by permission of Zondervan Publishing House. All from Biblegateway.com

PRINTED IN THE UNITED STATES OF AMERICA

What others are saying:

This book caused me to realize I still had unforgiveness towards a family member who molested me. After reading this book straight through, I then went back and did the daily reading and bible study. I can say that now and appreciating the rain and starting a new walk with God. MDavids…CA

In my 50 years on this earth I haven't read such an intimate personal devotional. I can't wait for the next one. Each and every scripture is perfect for the days reading and I loved getting my nuggets from the Lord…JCarter…MD

I did not expect to have Bible Study for 40 straight days! This was a pleasant and valued surprise……… C Smith…WI

Personal, powerful, precise. Thanks you for a deeper level. BWoods…PA

Thank you for your testimony, your witness, your survival. God is amazing and this book made me cry and laugh then praise and worship all at the same time. BBrown…GA

The addition of journal pages made me realize I hadn't written my thoughts down in many years. I looked forward to my daily journaling and decided to use this book as a 40 week devotional so I can go deeper into each of the scriptures and teachable moments. MCarter…TX

To God be the Glory

This book is lovingly dedicated to my late grandmother, Gladys Mae Spencer, the most influential person in my life. She instilled morals and values, and taught me discipline which has shaped and molded me into the person I am today.

Contents

Introduction		01

Day

1	First Date	08
2	New Beginnings	12
3	No Worries	15
4	Perseverance, Character & Hope	19
5	You have Authority	23
6	You are Not Alone	26
7	God is in Control	29
8	It's Your Time to Shine	33
9	Remember the Kingdom	36
10	The Selection Process	39
Prayer of Salvation		43
11	Falling into Grace	44
12	Rough Road Ahead	47
13	Be Strong and Very Courageous	50
14	When You Move I Move	54
15	Run and Don't Look Back	57
16	Speak Life	61
17	More of Him, Less of Me	65
18	Just do It	69
19	Never too Old or Young	73
20	The P.R.I.C.E. of Destiny	76
The Names of God		79
21	The P.U.R.S.U.I.T of Destiny	80
22	Do and Finish	83
23	The Battle is Not Yours	87
24	Just Stand	92
25	Take up Your Cross	96
26	Task Master	100
27	More Power	104
28	Never Satisfied	108
29	Heal My Finances	112
30	Wrap Me in Your Arms	116
Words of Encouragement		119

31 Everything I Need	. . . . .	120
32 Be Still		124
33 Use Your Tool Belt		128
34 Scales Falling from Your Eyes . .		132
35 Spiritual Urgency		136
36 My Tears, Your Tears		139
37 I Hear the Sound of Rain . . .		143
38 Increase in Faith and Patience . .		146
39 Trust God		150
40 40 Days and 40 Nights		154
Conclusion		158
Blank Journal Pages		160
About the **A**uthor		201

Introduction

"How about a nice long drive? Get some grapes, cheese, crackers, water, and juice. Let's take a drive and spend the day together like we used to. I love you so much and I miss spending time with you." I heard, "Just you and I, with no distractions, no cell phone, and no other person. Let's just drive until...until I tell you to stop. I miss our intimate time." Those words were like honey to my ears. So I packed grapes, nuts, cheese and crackers. I packed water and juice. I was sure to grab a few CD's for music to set the mood. I put on a classy but cute outfit and left the house picture perfect.

I stopped by my local gas station and got a full tank of gas. I was going on a date! I was so excited because it had been so long since we had done this. As I began to drive He told me to head south. I jumped on 95S heading away from Baltimore. The two of us. As I passed exits on the highway, I realized they all had memories of some sort. The many employers whom I had worked for over the years; the schools my daughter and I had attended; the family and friends who lived along various exits. And yes, all of the men I trusted and thought they were "the one" - but instead turned my life upside down and altered my path so many times. Choices, some good and some very bad, littered my mind as I drove. I didn't want to think of any of that right now.

This moment, I was on the perfect date, with the perfect mate, my man, my best friend and the lover of my soul! I was on a date with

Jesus! I crossed from Maryland to DC to Virginia and something happened. The air changed and became lighter. At some point He told me to stop driving, and then, I wrote the following journal entry:

"I am crying, I am crying hard...a freedom cry. I know major change is about to occur in my life, but where do I go and how do I get there? I've dreamed so many dreams and had so many words...Atlanta, GA, VA, FL, NY....where will this journey lead me God? I have read the Bible, I have prayed and I have fasted. I have been to Israel in the natural and every other country in the spirit. And yet today me and my tears sit in a parking lot in Annandale, VA which I do not doubt will become a part of my story. I've rededicated myself over and over, after each fall, after each victory. And today I know that you know I am yours. Always has been, always will be. Tell me Lord for your servant is listening. So Lord I wait patiently on the Lord, I wait on you I know you have heard my every plea, cry and my voice. Even the things I don't even think yet, you know. My date with Jesus - a book – who knew it would last lifetime." Hence we have:

The Perfect Date: A 40 day devotional and journal...a new Encounter with God

That was August of 2008. After I came back from VA I heard the Lord say write a book about these intimate dates and my relationship with the Lord. I ended that date by sitting up on Federal Hill in downtown Baltimore. I looked over the city; I watched people and I talked to God. I asked Him what He was saying. His reply came as He told me to open the pocket size

Bible in my hand. He said open it and the very page you open will be by response.

His response: Matthew 28:18-20 *"All authority in heaven and on earth has been given to me. Therefore go and make disciples of all nations, baptizing them in the name of the Father and of the Son and of the Holy Spirit, and teaching them to obey everything I have commanded you. And surely I am with you always, to the very end of the age." I will rejoice and be glad!*

Hence this devotional and journal are born. It has taken me over two years to actually sit down and attempt to complete it. I have started a thousand ways and on a thousand different days. I allowed delays and distractions, I allowed a lack of faith and fear, and I allowed procrastination and pain of the past to keep me from pursing purpose and completing the task.

This reminded me of a passage in Nehemiah 4:10-15 *"Meanwhile, the people in Judah said, 'the strength of the laborers is giving out, and there is so much rubble that we cannot rebuild the wall.' Also our enemies said, "Before they know it or see us, we will be right there among them and will kill them and put an end to the work." Then the Jews who lived near them came and told us ten times over, "Wherever you turn, they will attack us." Therefore I stationed some of the people behind the lowest points of the wall at the exposed places, posting them by families, with their swords, spears and bows. After I looked things over, I stood up and said to the nobles, the officials and the rest of the people, "Don't be afraid of them. Remember the*

Lord, who is great and awesome, and fight for your families, your sons and your daughters, your wives and your homes." When our enemies heard that we were aware of their plot and that God had frustrated it, we all returned to the wall, each to our own work."

What made today different you may ask? Yesterday I started a fast. I heard the Lord say "too much time has passed since you've fasted. You start today but on the days I tell you - drink only water. Do it until I tell you to stop." Well the funniest thing to me is that the following day was Thanksgiving! Yes, you read correctly Thanksgiving Day, and I had been invited to dinner and fellowship. They had already advised me of the menu....ham, turkey, yams, collard greens, string beans, macaroni and cheese, cabbage, cornbread, stuffing, cakes, pies and the list goes on. I thought to myself, I have got to be the only person on the planet who will be fasting on Thanksgiving Day; but as you know God is all wise and all knowing.

November 25, 2010, in my second day of the fast, drinking only water, this devotional was 90% completely written! Nobody but God knew it would take discipline in my flesh to birth out what is in my spirit. Nehemiah 1:4 *When I heard these things, I sat down and wept. For some days I mourned and fasted and prayed before the God of heaven.*

God desires to spend time with you. I saw a sign on a church once which read "If it seems like God is far away who moved." When was the last time you spent time with God? No cell phone, no email, no kids, no friends, no internet or facebook? When was the last time it was just you and Him?

The previous pages details one of many of my dates with the Master. Some I spent in Florida in beachfront hotels, some in places where lovers go like the Poconos. I went alone and yet I was not by myself. I went to be with my true Lover, my God. Many times I simply stayed at home cutting off my cell phone, the PC and spent time in my room. Other times I cleared out a walk in closet and I shut in and worshipped. I listened to worship music, I read the word, and sometimes I did nothing, but the one thing I did do - I waited on the Lord. He always speaks. Do not rush Him or put Him on your time table or schedule.

God desires for us to minister to Him the same way they did in the Bible:

- *David did in Psalm 63:8 when he cried out to God "My soul follows hard after you."*
- *Joshua 13:14 states "But to the tribe of Levi he gave no inheritance, since the food offerings presented to the LORD, the God of Israel, are their inheritance, as he promised them."*
- *Acts 13:2 states "As they ministered to the Lord, and fasted, the Holy Ghost said, separate me Barnabas and Saul for the work whereunto I have called them."*

I challenge you for the next 40 days to seek His face and minister unto the Father. Every question, every decision, every need you have,

God will provide answers, directions and resources. He will meet you right where you are. This journey will bring you up to a higher level and a deeper place in living out the will of God.

Each day begin by reading the scripture and devotional, and then write your journal entry to Him. I have added space directly under each day's reading and I have also added several additional journal pages in the back of the book. Journal entries should convey what is in your heart by being totally honest with God. Tell Him how you are really feeling, what you really need, and what you are feeling and hearing Him say to you.

Each day begin by:

- Setting time aside each day - strictly as your time with God.
- Praying throughout the day.
- Asking for forgiveness.
- Expecting and seeking a new encounter with God.
- Being open to the newness He wants to bring in your life including the new revelation of who He is.
- Reading the assigned passage(s) of scripture.
- Writing the revelation or nugget you received from the Lord while completing the reading for the day.
- Writing the revelation(s) from the assigned scripture reading.
- Writing and end with a targeted prayer focus.

- Committing to a lifetime of Dates with Jesus!

We want so many things from God. Too often we want what is in His hand, but I assure you, if you seek diligently after His heart, you will discover a sweeter place in Him. He only wants you!

Day 1 ~ First Date
~ Read John 15
Scripture focus: John 15:1-4

I am the true vine, and my Father is the gardener. He cuts off every branch in me that bears no fruit, while every branch that does bear fruit he prunes so that it will be even more fruitful. You are already clean because of the word I have spoken to you. Remain in me, as I also remain in you. No branch can bear fruit by itself; it must remain in the vine. Neither can you bear fruit unless you remain in me.

~**M**y very first dates with Jesus started when I was a little girl. Yes, I used to play with dolls, play dress up, and have tea time. Yes, I talked to my imaginary friends, but I remember talking to God as early as I can remember. I would talk to Him about anything and everything. I would talk to Him while walking down the street smiling and laughing. This behavior lasted through the years. Many times I wondered about the things in everyday life, but most of the time I would just talk to God like I did my mother or grandmother.

I remember one incident in particular. I had come home from elementary school and as usual I was starving. I placed my book bag in its designated spot and went into the kitchen to retrieve my after school sandwich and snack. I looked outside and saw my grandmother in the back yard pruning her rose bush. I said to God "Wow how do you feed the roses, is it like you feed me." I heard just as plain as day, "Yes, I feed the roses just as I feed you. I will always feed you and take care of you."

My grandmother was pruning the rose bush to:

- Encourage new growth
- Remove dead wood
- Improve air circulation
- Shape the plant

Likewise, our Father has to prune us and He is the only gardener who has all authority to do so. Like the rose bush, we all have to be encouraged to continue growing in the things of God to reach full bloom which is destiny. During this process God removes the dead weight from us. Sometimes this is in the form of people, material possessions, or through self examination, which leads to true repentance. Once this process has been completed, we are in position to receive a fresh breath, a fresh word, and a fresh revelation from our Lord and Savior. Finally, He shapes and molds us to look just like Him!

Then God said, "Let us make mankind in our image, in our likeness... So God created mankind in his own image, in the image of God he created them; male and female he created them. Genesis 1:26-27

Date: Time:

Journal Entry:

Write the nugget you received from the Lord while completing the reading for today.

_____
_____
_____
_____
_____
_____
_____
_____
_____
_____
_____
_____
_____
_____

Scripture Reading: Personal revelation today?

_____

Prayer focus:

Day 2 ~ New Beginnings
~ Read Genesis 1
Scripture focus: Genesis 1:1-2

In the beginning God created the heaven and the earth. And the earth was without form, and void; and darkness was upon the face of the deep. And the Spirit of God moved upon the face of the waters.

~**N**ew beginnings are always a time filled with excitement and joy for the most part, but many also experience fear and doubt. We often find ourselves wondering if we have truly made the right choice. You may be reading this and you have never given your life to Christ; today is a great day to start your new beginning. (See page 43 for the prayer of Salvation) For others, your new beginning may be leaving a job to start a new one, going from singleness to marriage, divorce to singleness, recovering from an addiction, grieving the death of a loved one, or simply coming back to God. Whatever the situation, we typically have a variety of emotions and many people often feel a void during various times of transition.

Rest assured feeling a void is normal and the good news is that our Lord and Savior Jesus Christ is the only one who can fill the void. I dare you today to go on your first date, or seek a new encounter with Him. He will speak peace and give you confidence as you begin this new journey.

Date: Time:

Journal Entry:

Write the nugget you received from the Lord while completing the reading for today.

_____
_____
_____
_____
_____
_____
_____
_____
_____
_____
_____
_____

Scripture Reading: Personal revelation today?

Prayer focus:

Day 3 ~ No Worries
~ Read Matthew 6
Scripture focus: Matthew 6:25-34

Therefore I tell you, do not worry about your life, what you will eat or drink; or about your body, what you will wear. Is not life more than food, and the body more than clothes? Look at the birds of the air; they do not sow or reap or store away in barns, and yet your heavenly Father feeds them. Are you not much more valuable than they? Can any one of you by worrying add a single hour to your life? And why do you worry about clothes? See how the flowers of the field grow. They do not labor or spin...Therefore do not worry about tomorrow, for tomorrow will worry about itself. Each day has enough trouble of its own.

~It's easier said than done! While meditating on this scripture we realize "not worrying" is easier said than done. Most of us find ourselves worried about everything including our children, our jobs, the economy, health issues, and the list goes on and on. One thing I have found to be true is that when I do not spend enough time with God, in His presence, and in His word, I worry. I faced foreclosure a few years back and anyone who has experienced this knows how stressful of an event it is. I was unemployed at the time and behind on my car payment. I cried, I worried, I wondered where I was going to lay my head, and how in the world I was going to come up with the money needed to keep my house. Then, one day when it became obvious that saving my house was not going to happen, I heard that still small voice tell me it was time for a date in a special meeting place.

I cleared out the walk in closet in my bedroom. I turned off my cell phone, grabbed my Bible, my journal, and a CD player. I went in the closet and turned off the lights to avoid any distractions, and then I cried. I cried for what seemed to be hours because at that moment I couldn't pray. Then, I turned on the light and read the scripture for today; I just turned right to it! I heard God loud and clear, "Do not worry." I began to pray which led me into worship. I spent my days and nights in that closet for six weeks straight. When I was not taking care of business, or eating, I was in the closet. I found peace, I found faith, and I found strength in that closet.

I received the paperwork and date to vacate the premises. I went to the closet for the final days in my house and understood clearly that I had to trust God. I came out of the closet victorious to the point where I said "if I have to go live with family or in a shelter, God will keep me." Within seven days of handing over the keys to the property, God gave me a job and an apartment to call home!

But my eyes are toward You, O God the Lord; in You do I trust and take refuge; pour not out my life nor leave it destitute and bare. Psalm 141:8

Date: Time:

Journal Entry:

Write the nugget you received from the Lord while completing the reading for today.

_____

_____

_____

_____

_____

_____

_____

_____

_____

_____

_____

_____

_____

_____

Scripture Reading: Personal revelation today?

_____

_____

_____

_____

_____

_____

_____

_____

_____

_____

Prayer focus:

_____

_____

_____

_____

_____

Day 4 ~ Perseverance, Character & Hope ~ Read Romans 5
Scripture focus: Romans 5:1-5

Therefore, since we have been justified through faith, we have peace with God through our Lord Jesus Christ, through whom we have gained access by faith into this grace in which we now stand. And we boast in the hope of the glory of God. Not only so, but we also glory in our sufferings, because we know that suffering produces perseverance, perseverance, character and character, hope. And hope does not put us to shame, because God's love has been poured out into our hearts through the Holy Spirit, who has been given to us.

~Have you ever really thought about what those three words really mean? Well allow me to give you the definitions:
- **Perseverance** - steady persistence in a course of action, a purpose, a state, etc., esp. in spite of difficulties, obstacles, or discouragement.
- **Character** - the aggregate of features and traits that form the individual nature of some person or thing.
- **Hope** - to look forward to with desire and reasonable confidence.

The truth of the matter is that I could not give you those definitions without giving you one more.
- **Suffering** - to undergo, be subjected to, or endure (pain, distress, injury, loss, or anything unpleasant.

Suffering can begin at any time and does not care about your age, race, gender, or your economic status. Suffering comes in many forms – emotional, physical, mental, financial, and even spiritual.

I remember being in a relationship years ago and feeling rejected the entire time. Nothing I did or said was ever good enough. I heard the word "no" one too many times. I was lied to and humiliated in front of others. God gave me the strength, fortitude, and perseverance to leave that relationship. Afterwards, I suffered a great deal for several reasons. I walked around with the spirit of rejection for many years. In my mind this one person did not want me, so nobody wanted me. Out of this and many other experiences, it was then that my true spiritual character emerged, and I loved it. Then, I thought how Jesus Christ suffered on a cross and paid the ultimate price for me. I began to forgive and seek forgiveness; I began to hope again, I began to breathe again.

Whatever situation you are facing today remember "we have gained access by faith into this grace in which we now stand. And we boast in the hope of the glory of God." In Him we are made whole, in Him we are set free from the pain and rejection of this world.

Date: Time:

Journal Entry:

Write the nugget you received from the Lord while completing the reading for today.

_____
_____
_____
_____
_____
_____
_____
_____
_____
_____
_____
_____

Scripture Reading: Personal revelation today?

_____
_____

_____
_____
_____
_____
_____
_____
_____
_____

Prayer focus:

_____
_____
_____
_____
_____
_____

Day 5 ~ You have Authority
~ Read Hebrews 1 and 2
Scripture focus: Hebrews 2:6-8

What is mankind that you are mindful of them, a son of man that you care for him? You made them a little lower than the angels; you crowned them with glory and honor and put everything under their feet.

~I have had the opportunity to speak and minister to many people across this country. One thing that I have found to be true is the fact that many people are living beneath their potential and living in a defeated manner. Some people have lost hope, joy, and the will to survive. Others have been broken and disappointed so many times in their lives that they feel like "what is the point of trying" and they never try anything else. We sit back and watch everyone else succeed and achieve their dreams, but yet we do not. Many times people get stuck in a place of pain, fear and rejection, and they cannot move forward. These are the times when you must dig deep and encourage yourself. God is so concerned about us. He also knows when we are not able to encourage ourselves, and then He will send someone to push us, motivate us, and help us go forth.

The Word explains that "God made us a little lower than the angels...and put everything under their feet." You have authority, why are you not using it? Just think how wonderful you feel after an achievement. Now think of the difference if you were to challenge yourself, and change your mindset to understand who you are, and that you walk in God given authority, how much more could you achieve in this lifetime!

I can do all this through him who gives me strength. Philippians 4:13

Date: Time:

Journal Entry:

Write the nugget you received from the Lord while completing the reading for today.

_____

_____

_____

_____

_____

_____

_____

_____

_____

_____

_____

_____

_____

Scripture Reading: Personal revelation today?

_____

_____

_____

_____

_____

_____

_____

Prayer focus:

_____

_____

_____

_____

Day 6 ~ You are Not Alone
~ Read Mark 9
Scripture focus: Mark 9:2

After six days Jesus took Peter, James and John with him and led them up a high mountain, where they were all alone. There he was transfigured before them.

~Have you ever been to a restaurant alone? I have on several occasions and is it just me or do people stare at you like you are crazy, or like they feel sorry for you? Many times the waiter or waitress will even try to hold polite conversation in an effort to help you not feel alone. Once, I even had a waitress sit down and begin to tell me her life story. Did anyone ever stop to think maybe I was at dinner alone because I wanted to be? On one of my recent dates, I went to a fancy restaurant with my journal in hand. The restaurant, unbeknown to me, was having some sort of special and the place was packed. I had to wait an hour or so for a table but I knew this was where I was supposed to be. Once my name was called they sat me at what seemed like the biggest booth style table in the restaurant. Immediately, I started receiving the pity stares!

I ignored them and after making my dining selection began to sit and talk to God - not out loud, of course, or they really would have taken me away. I listened more than I spoke. Then, I began to write in my journal.

There have been and will continue to be many days when we are alone but not lonely. I want to assure you, God is with you, and He wants this alone time so He can show Himself to you. He wants to show you who you are in Him and show you various aspects of His character with each new encounter. Embrace your time alone with the Master.

...I will never leave thee, nor forsake thee. Hebrews 13:5

Date: Time:

Journal Entry:

Write the nugget you received from the Lord while completing the reading for today.

_____

_____

_____

_____

_____

_____

_____

_____

_____

_____

_____

Scripture Reading: Personal revelation today?

_____

_____

_____

_____

_____

_____

_____

Prayer focus:

_____

_____

_____

_____

Day 7 ~ God is in Control
~ Read Mark 4
Scripture focus: Mark 4:35 - 41

That day when evening came, he said to his disciples, "Let us go over to the other side." Leaving the crowd behind, they took him along, just as he was, in the boat. There were also other boats with him. A furious squall came up, and the waves broke over the boat, so that it was nearly swamped. Jesus was in the stern, sleeping on a cushion. The disciples woke him and said to him, "Teacher, don't you care if we drown?" He got up, rebuked the wind and said to the waves, "Quiet! Be still!" Then the wind died down and it was completely calm. He said to his disciples, "Why are you so afraid? Do you still have no faith?" They were terrified and asked each other, "Who is this? Even the wind and the waves obey him!"

~**W**hen my daughter was in middle school we were in a car accident. The morning was like many mornings before. It started with us waking up; getting dressed, eating breakfast, and then we were out the door. The weather was cold and rainy as a frost had come the night before. I drove the same way I had driven daily and I expected a routine trip. Upon nearing her school we had one light to go and then it happened. I saw the light turning yellow and began to slow down and brake. My car didn't stop and I ran into the back of an SUV. Once I got out of my car, I realized that this patch of ground had a few icy patches, and that my tires did not have enough traction to conquer the ice.

I was not in control of the weather, the tires, nor was I in control of anything else that morning. I understood then, as I do now, that God is always in control. Storms of life including accidents, death, divorce, a health crisis, or a financial crisis will happen. We can try to hit the brakes, or think we are going to continue living our routine lives, but life has other plans. Some storms we can see coming ahead of time and we are able to brace for them, while others are totally unexpected. Just as Jesus spoke to the storm then, He speaks to your storm now: "Peace, Be still." God desires to give and restore your peace in the midst of the storm. He is the only one who can truly comfort you during such turbulent times. Will you be still long enough to allow Him to be your Peace and the Lord of your life? I dare you to give Him complete control!

Date: Time:

Journal Entry:

Write the nugget you received from the Lord while completing the reading for today.

_____

_____

_____

_____

_____

_____
_____
_____
_____
_____
_____
_____
_____
_____
_____
_____

Scripture Reading: Personal revelation today?

_____
_____
_____
_____
_____

Prayer focus:

Day 8 ~ It's Your Time to Shine
~ Read John 1
Scripture focus: John 1:1-5

In the beginning was the Word, and the Word was with God, and the Word was God. The same was in the beginning with God. All things were made by him; and without him was not any thing made that was made. In him was life; and the life was the light of men. And the light shineth in darkness; and the darkness comprehended it not.

~One thing is very apparent on this journey we call life: Everyone has a time to shine! The question is why do so many procrastinate or not take advantage of the time? Dreams and visions are on the inside of you waiting to come out. How do I know, because the word for today states "All things were made by him." God creates, He is the creator and because we are made in his likeness, you have creativity on the inside of you. Many of us find ourselves in situations and around people who kill the light on the inside of us. You have a choice to stay in darkness, depression, doubt and despair, or allow your light to shine! Once you make this choice you may lose friends, and family may distance themselves because as the Word states "And the light shineth in darkness; and the darkness comprehended it not." It is not your job to make someone understand what God is doing in your life. It is your job to complete the vision on the inside of you.

God has appointed and anointed you in this dispensation of time to shine! Go forth to write the book, produce the CD, preach the sermon, discover the mission field, start a blog, or go back to school! Whatever vision God has placed on the inside of you, He will also be your guiding light to help it come to pass.

Your word is a lamp for my feet, a light on my path.
Psalm 119:105

Date: Time:

Journal Entry:

Write the nugget you received from the Lord while completing the reading for today.

_____

_____

_____

_____

_____

_____

_____

_____

_____

_____

_____

_____

Scripture Reading: Personal revelation today?

_____

_____

_____

_____

_____

_____

_____

Prayer focus:

_____

_____

_____

_____

_____

Day 9 ~ Remember the Kingdom
~ Read Matthew 6
Scripture focus: Matthew 6:9-13

This, then, is how you should pray: Our Father in heaven, hallowed be your name, your kingdom come, your will be done, on earth as it is in heaven. Give us today our daily bread. And forgive us our debts, as we also have forgiven our debtors. And lead us not into temptation, but deliver us from the evil one.

~There are several scripture references to the Kingdom throughout the Bible. The Kingdom of God is the rule of an eternal sovereign God over all creatures and things. What does this mean to us? You have to believe and understand that God is eternal, sovereign, all wise, and all knowing. Once we know this, we truly begin to make different choices because we understand God knows what is best for us. Every closed door was closed for a reason and for our protection although we can't see it at the time. Just as He closes doors, He also opens doors. However, all doors are not opened by God; some the enemy opens and others we open ourselves.

Once we understand the Kingdom principle, we can then operate in the will of God. When it comes to the will of God, we have to be willing to walk in it, and walk it out. This can only come when you constantly pray and read the Word of God while asking Him for direction. The will of God leads to us living heavenly lives right here on earth! The scripture for today says:

- First: your kingdom come
- Second: your will be done
- Third: on earth as it is in heaven

So, please do remember the Kingdom today. Remember that God's precepts and principles are your roadmap each and every day.

The LORD has established his throne in heaven, and his kingdom rules over all. Psalm 103:19

Date: Time:

Journal Entry:

Write the nugget you received from the Lord while completing the reading for today.

_____

_____

_____

_____

_____

_____

_____

_____

Scripture Reading: Personal revelation today?

Prayer focus:

Day 10 ~ The Selection Process
~ Read 1 Peter 2
Scripture focus: 1 Peter 2:9

But you are a chosen race, a royal priesthood, a dedicated nation, [God's] own purchased, special people, that you may set forth the wonderful deeds and display the virtues and perfections of Him Who called you out of darkness into His marvelous light.

~**G**oing out to the schoolyard for recess was the best part of the day during my youth. I loved to play, but I hated when it was time for a team activity. There would be two groups and two team captains. The team captains had the chore of selecting or choosing who they thought would help them win the game of the day. It was the worst feeling when I was the last or next to the last person selected. As I have gone through life, I have realized over time that the schoolyard experience was preparing me for the cruel world that we can sometimes live in. Whether it was a promotion that I deserved and did not get, being turned down for an apartment, or even not being selected for something in church, those childhood memories stayed with me.

On one of my dates with Jesus, I wanted to go away and spend a few days with Him. I prayed and chose to go to the Pocono Mountains in Pennsylvania. I drove from MD to PA. What should have been an easy trip turned out to be quite adventurous. Instead of taking the main highway, I had the bright idea to take the scenic route. This was before the GPS was popular and affordable so I had nothing but a printed map and directions from my computer. I was lost and driving so slow at one point until I was pulled over by the police. Once I made it to my destination I spent the next four days and three nights seeking God, praying, reading the Word, and listening. I had recently applied for a job that was very important to me, but I was not selected. Once again I felt like I did as a child, as if I was not good enough for somebody's team. I asked God why I was not chosen. God began to speak to me saying "He chose me before the foundation of the earth, before I was formed in my mother's womb. I had been called out of darkness, sin and certain death into the marvelous light." I felt so special that day to come into the realization that when God chose me, nothing else mattered, nothing else compared and nothing else would ever make me feel less than "a chosen race, a royal priesthood." You have been selected and you are chosen by God!

Date: Time:

Journal Entry:

Write the nugget you received from the Lord while completing the reading for today.

_____

_____

_____

Scripture Reading: Personal revelation today?

Prayer focus:

Prayer of Salvation

"Dear Heavenly Father, I acknowledge to You that I am a sinner. I believe that Your Son Jesus Christ shed His blood on the cross, died for my sins, and rose again on the third day. I am sorry for the sins which I have committed against You, and I am willing to turn away from my sins. Cleanse me, and forgive me of my sins as I forgive anyone who has ever sinned against me.

Right now I confess Jesus as the Lord of my life. With my heart, I believe that God the Father raised His Son Jesus from the dead. This very moment I acknowledge that Jesus Christ is my Savior and according to His Word, right now I am born again.

Thank You, Jesus, for coming into my life and hearing my prayer. I ask all of this in the name of my Lord and Savior, Jesus Christ. Amen."

Day 11 ~ Falling into Grace
~ Read Jude
Scripture focus: Jude 24-25

Now to Him Who is able to keep you without stumbling or slipping or falling, and to present [you] unblemished (blameless and faultless) before the presence of His glory in triumphant joy and exultation [with unspeakable, ecstatic delight]--To the one only God, our Savior through Jesus Christ our Lord, be glory (splendor), majesty, might and dominion, and power and authority, before all time and now and forever (unto all the ages of eternity). Amen (so be it).

~**D**oubt, fear, lack, greed, lust, envy, finances, and a lack of faith are just a few reasons which can cause a person to fall. We watch the news, and know of people personally, who have fallen in a public forum. There are thousands and thousands more who fall in private in the privacy of their homes. These are the ones who names we will never know, where they live, what church they attend, or their walk with God. We do not see the smoking, drinking, fornication, marital affairs, lying, cheating and stealing. Nor do we see the many addictions like gambling, shopping, or pornography to name a few.

If you have found yourself in a fallen state it is never too late to ask God for forgiveness. The word states in Proverbs 24:16a "For a righteous *man* may fall seven times and rise again..." If you repent and turn away from that sin, God "is able to keep you without stumbling or slipping or falling, and to present [you] unblemished (blameless and faultless) before the presence of His glory in triumphant joy and exultation [with unspeakable, ecstatic delight]." In other words you can go from falling into sin to Falling into Grace!

Date: Time:

Journal Entry:

Write the nugget you received from the Lord while completing the reading for today.

_____

_____

_____

_____

_____

_____

_____

_____

_____

Scripture Reading: Personal revelation today?

Prayer focus:

Day 12 ~ Rough Road Ahead
~ Read Isaiah 43
Scripture focus: Isaiah 43:19

I am going to do something new. It is already happening. Don't you recognize it? I will clear a way in the desert. I will make rivers on dry land.

~I was driving and saw a sign as they were tearing up, then fixing the street. I had ridden on this street many times and was glad to see the repairs finally happening. This particular sign was orange with black lettering and it caught my attention. It read "Rough Road Ahead." I thought to myself that's what they should tell you when you give you life to Christ... Rough Road Ahead followed by the next sign which read "Road Under Construction."

Just like that road, sometimes we have to be torn up from our old ways, mindsets, tradition, and religious thinking. God has to take out the old and make us like Him so that we are truly a new creature in Christ. Once we give our life to Christ, it does not mean everything is going to be easy, nor does it mean that the road ahead will be smooth. What it does mean, is that we now depend on God, trust God, and have peace even in the most stressful times of our lives. We have our most important date with Him when we accept the Lord as our personal Savior and Lord over our lives. The walk with Jesus truly lasts a lifetime. You are headed in the right direction! It's a rough road ahead but it's the best road ahead!

Date: Time:

Journal Entry:

Write the nugget you received from the Lord while completing the reading for today.

_____

_____

_____

_____

_____

_____

_____

_____

_____

_____

_____

_____

_____

Scripture Reading: Personal revelation today?

Prayer focus:

Day 13 ~ Be Strong and Very Courageous
~ Read Joshua 1
Scripture focus: Joshua 1:7-9

Be strong and very courageous. Be careful to obey all the law my servant Moses gave you; do not turn from it to the right or to the left, that you may be successful wherever you go. Keep this Book of the Law always on your lips; meditate on it day and night, so that you may be careful to do everything written in it. Then you will be prosperous and successful. Have I not commanded you? Be strong and courageous. Do not be afraid; do not be discouraged, for the LORD your God will be with you wherever you go.

~"You are pregnant." As I heard the doctor say those words to me, I had no immediate reaction. Then, fear gripped my fourteen year old body. I was turning fifteen that summer and had only had sex a few times. I didn't understand. I had asked my parents and grandparents for birth control months before, but they all said the same thing, "You are too young for sex." So I tried it a few times thinking I would get birth control at some point. My family was devastated at hearing the news. I went through the pregnancy with little support. In my seventh month I slipped on a rug and fell. I went to the doctors and they gave me a good report.

I had a dream that night that my baby was still born. The doctors continued to give me a good report throughout the pregnancy. Having reached full term, I went into labor and at some point I saw the panic on the doctors faces. Then they broke the news to me: "the baby has died inside of you." I still had to complete labor and delivery knowing I would not have a baby to take home with me. I delivered a 7lb baby and was told a blood clot had formed in the umbilical cord suddenly during labor and the baby did not receive oxygen.

I will never know if it was my fall at seven months that caused the still birth, or if it was really as the doctors stated. What I do know is that the grief I experienced at fifteen was unbearable, unspeakable, and undeniable. Of the several visitors I received at the hospital, one of them was the new Pastor at my church. He came with prayer and with a Bible. He said quietly "the Lord will comfort you." The night before I was scheduled to be discharged, I picked up that Bible. I had one before but I had never really read it. I opened the Bible and turned to today's scripture focus. "Be strong and courageous. Do not be afraid; do not be discouraged, for the LORD your God will be with you wherever you go." I read those words over and over again until one day many months later, I didn't feel pain. I felt what I now know to be the peace that surpasses all understanding.

If you have suffered a loss please go through the grieving process. There is no right or wrong way and the tears will come. Do not be hard on yourself and be very careful not to get stuck there. Through God, you will have the strength to live and live one day at a time. Be strong and very courageous says the Lord.

+++

Date: Time:

Journal Entry:

Write the nugget you received from the Lord while completing the reading for today.

Scripture Reading: Personal revelation today?

Prayer focus:

Day 14 ~ When You Move I Move
~ Read Exodus 40
Scripture focus: Exodus 40:36-38

In all the travels of the Israelites, whenever the cloud lifted from above the tabernacle, they would set out; but if the cloud did not lift, they did not set out—until the day it lifted. So the cloud of the LORD was over the tabernacle by day, and fire was in the cloud by night, in the sight of all the Israelites during all their travels.

~Have you ever felt out of sort, out of place, or ahead of your time? There have been many seasons in my life where I wondered why was I here, what was my purpose, and was I really in the right place at the right time. When those questions arose and often times seem to consume me, I knew it was time to go on a date with Jesus. One such time, God had moved me across several state lines into unfamiliar territory. I was away from family and friends and I was straight out of my comfort zone. I had to learn the lay of the land from the local grocery store, to the post office, to the church I would be attending. There were a few days where things did not go smoothly and I began to question God. I locked myself in the house, shut off all methods of communication with the outside world, and began to seek the face of God.

During this quiet time before God, I heard the Lord say "Do not worry, when you move I move because when I asked you to move you were obedient." We have to be like the Israelites who did not move unless God moved.

Do not make rash or hurried choices. Wait on God and when He moves or tells you to move, then and only then should you do so. If He is silent, or you do not feel you have received clear, concise direction, then do not move. The Lord will move on your behalf when you have sought the Lord, when you trust the Lord, and when you follow Him.

Date: Time:

Journal Entry:

Write the nugget you received from the Lord while completing the reading for today.

_____

_____

_____

_____

_____

_____

_____

_____

Scripture Reading: Personal revelation today?

Prayer focus:

Day 15 ~ Run and Don't Look Back!
~ Read Genesis 19
Scripture focus: Genesis 19:21-26

He said to him, "Very well, I will grant this request too; I will not overthrow the town you speak of. But flee there quickly, because I cannot do anything until you reach it. By the time Lot reached Zoar, the sun had risen over the land. Then the LORD rained down burning sulfur on Sodom and Gomorrah—from the LORD out of the heavens. Thus he overthrew those cities and the entire plain, destroying all those living in the cities—and also the vegetation in the land. But Lot's wife looked back, and she became a pillar of salt.

~**R**un and don't look back! Those were the words from my sister years ago when I found myself in an unhealthy relationship. I had been involved with a person who was very controlling, dominating and manipulating. I had never been intimate with this man, nor had I really dated him as two people normally date. I worked with this man and allowed him to slowly but surely seduce my mind. He had me convinced that I was the one and that he loved me. You know that thing that women have, that alerts you and warns you, that something isn't right, it was screaming at me, but I chose to ignore it. That is until so many red flags were thrown in my face until I could no longer live in denial. I discovered in the course of a few hours who this man truly was, inside and out. I discovered several other women who thought they were the one too!

I was traumatized to say the least because this was the first time a man had played with my mind. Others had played with my heart but this....this was totally different. I really felt like I was losing my mind. I would see things with my own eyes and he would tell me I didn't see it to a point where I started to believe it. When it was all said and done my sister said to me "you need to run and don't look back."

So needless to say the mind games left me a nervous wreck, which eventually led to a nervous breakdown, medication, and therapy. I knew God, but I allowed my desire and need for attention, love, and loneliness lead me to the depths of despair. I had a few similar experiences in church as well which left me with "church hurt." There are many types of unhealthy relationships. Some may be abusive physically, mentally, emotionally or spiritually. These relationships take place in our families, on our jobs, in our churches, and in our society. You are important and loved by God. You have heard that still small voice telling you to run and don't look back. God will deliver you if you want to be delivered, and when He does - don't look back!

Date: Time:

Journal Entry:

Write the nugget you received from the Lord while completing the reading for today.

Scripture Reading: Personal revelation today?

Prayer focus:

Day 16 ~ Speak Life
~ Read Acts 2
Scripture focus: Acts 2:17-21

In the last days, God says, I will pour out my Spirit on all people. Your sons and daughters will prophesy, your young men will see visions, your old men will dream dreams. Even on my servants, both men and women, I will pour out my Spirit in those days, and they will prophesy...And everyone who calls on the name of the Lord will be saved.

~**As** a little girl I loved to play with the boys in the neighborhood. I liked to shoot marbles, play tag football, and ride my big wheel. My grandmother used to call me a tom boy. On one occasion, I was playing on a train track type of bridge that ran across the top of several streets in my neighborhood. I had been warned not to ever go up there. One of the boys in the neighborhood challenged me and said I was a girl and I was too scared to climb up the path that led to the top. I had a dream a few days prior in which a little girl was caught on a high wire like they use at the circus. The girl stood there and didn't know what to do so she said "Jesus help me." Just then, a helicopter appeared, and the girl climbed aboard to safety.

I chose to ignore all of my ten years of wisdom, and the strict instructions from my grandmother. I began to climb, and if you have ever seen one of these bridges, you know, they are not meant for climbing. I made it to the top but had to get down on the other side. The boy climbed halfway down and then he jumped. I stood there wondering how I was going to get out of this one. I tried to climb down, but instead, I fell. I landed on an old mattress that had been discarded, but I could not see it from where I was on the bridge. I fell and I know it was the hand of God that kept me from hitting the concrete ground. If only God had kept me from the wrath of my grandmother when she heard about it, but that's another story.

At the tender age of ten I didn't realize my dream was a warning not to climb up on that bridge. It would be many years later as an adult until I even remembered the incident, the dream and the revelation. I have always known things, seen things and dreamed many dreams. There were many dreams and visions that I never told a soul about only to watch them come to pass shortly thereafter. If you are reading this and saying "wow that's me" - God desires to speak to you even more, and to have intimate fellowship with you. God will show you things in a vision, or dream concerning you and your family – it is for protection and direction. Pray and Speak Life to it!

✝✝✝

Date: Time:

Journal Entry:

Write the nugget you received from the Lord while completing the reading for today.

_____

_____

Scripture Reading: Personal revelation today?

Prayer focus:

Day 17 ~ More of Him, Less of Me
~ Read Matthew 5
Scripture focus: Matthew 5:6

Blessed are those who hunger and thirst for righteousness, for they will be filled.

~I love cheesecake, chicken and pizza. I could eat some or all of these items everyday. If I am totally honest, I love food. Unfortunately, as I have gotten older, I have come to love food more than I should. I woke one day to realize that I was an emotional eater. I ate when I was hungry, happy, sad, stressed out, and the list goes on and on. I began to seek God. I read the Word to gain strength to turn down my plate, and fight my addiction to food. I began to fast and pray, and discovered several things. Fasting truly can break addictions. I discovered many root causes to my addiction and how I had began to turn to food for comfort. One of the most important things I discovered during fasting was my true desperate need and hunger for God. I didn't want to watch television or even be on the computer. I didn't want to talk on the phone or send a text message. I wanted God! I wanted, needed, and craved more of God. I wanted a new encounter, a new worship experience, and I wanted to stay in His presence.

How do you do that? How do you work, take care of your family, take care of yourself and get to a new place in God? I am glad you asked because I have a few answers for you! There are several ways, but I found that they all had to be combined daily in one way or another:

- Earnestly seek Him with your whole heart.
- Be honest and tell Him how you really feel, and what you are really struggling with.
- Admit that you are a sinner and ask for forgiveness daily (Forgive others as well)
- Read the Word every day, even when you do not feel like it.
- Pray and talk to God throughout the day.
- Listen to sermons and worship music as often as possible.
- Do not talk to negative or draining people.
- Do not tell the things, that God reveals to you, to just anyone.
- Decrease so that He can truly Increase
- Stand in expectation, by faith!

I found that on days when I tried to do as many of these throughout my day, God truly made time for everything else. I discovered my attitude and thought process became different when dealing with people and situations. More of Him means less of me, which means, More of Him!

Date: Time:

Journal Entry:

Write the nugget you received from the Lord while completing the reading for today.

Scripture Reading: Personal revelation today?

Prayer focus:

Day 18 ~ Just do It
~ Read Habakkuk 2
Scripture focus: Habakkuk 2:2-3

Write down the revelation and make it plain on tablets so that a herald may run with it. For the revelation awaits an appointed time; it speaks of the end and will not prove false. Though it linger, wait for it; will certainly come and will not delay.

~Anyone can do any amount of work, provided it isn't the work he is supposed to be doing at that moment. ~Robert Benchley

As I read that quote, I laughed because it described most people I know so well. The people who are good at telling others what to do but haven't done what they are supposed to be doing. There is a word for this – Procrastination (To put off intentionally and habitually) – have you heard of it?

If you are like me, I am good at helping other people pursue and achieve their visions and dreams. However, when it comes to me, I tend to procrastinate. I have asked myself many times why do I do this. The answers were sometimes complex and other times quite simple. I had a fear of failure and a fear of success. I had a fear of rejection and a fear of acceptance. I harbored many memories of past failures, defeats, and let downs. I had an epiphany a few years ago that if I never even wrote the vision, I would not receive provision. If I never moved forward past my past, I would stay in the past. I began to understand seasons and times, and that I was losing both by doing nothing.

I heard God begin to tell me to "Just do it and I have your back." The most amazing things began to happen. All of that mess and garbage from my past was being dealt with in the things God was telling me to do. People around me were even more inspired to see me fulfill my purpose, and most importantly I began to feel inspired and encouraged. The Word says "Write down the revelation and make it plain on tablets so that a herald may run with it. For the revelation awaits an appointed time; it speaks of the end and will not prove false. Though it linger, wait for it; will certainly come and will not delay." What are you waiting for – Just do it, He has your Back!

Date: Time:

Journal Entry:

Write the nugget you received from the Lord while completing the reading for today.

_____

_____

_____

_____

_____

_____

_____

_____

_____

_____

_____

_____

_____

_____

_____

Scripture Reading: Personal revelation today?

_____

_____

_____

_____

_____

_____

Prayer focus:

Day 19 ~ Never too Old or Young
~ Read Jeremiah 1
Scripture focus: Jeremiah 1:4-8

The word of the LORD came to me, saying, "Before I formed you in the womb I knew you, before you were born I set you apart; I appointed you as a prophet to the nations." "Alas, Sovereign LORD," I said, "I do not know how to speak; I am too young." But the LORD said to me, "Do not say, 'I am too young.' You must go to everyone I send you to and say whatever I command you. Do not be afraid of them, for I am with you and will rescue you," declares the LORD.

~One of the many things that I love about God is that He will choose and use whosoever He calls. Romans 2:11 states: "For there is no partiality with God." It does not matter whether you are nine or ninety nine; it is never too late to serve God. We read of many instances in the Bible where God defies man's thoughts and concept of age. Sarah conceiving at the age of 90; Moses called to lead at the age of 80; Aaron was 83...you see where I am going.

I was 29 when I got the call to preach the Gospel and 40 when I was called to Pastor a church in San Antonio, TX. I thought I was too young to do both, but God; He is the only one who can get the Glory. I have had many say what I can't do, or what I shouldn't do, but Glory to God that He is truly no respecter of person. This includes my gender, my race, my age and my socio economic status. God is concerned with my heart and my walk. Maybe

you are reading this and someone has told you that you were too old or too young; too rich or too poor, or that you can't or won't because your father or mother didn't. The word says "Do not say, 'I am too young.' You must go to everyone I send you to and say whatever I command you. Do not be afraid of them, for I am with you and will rescue you," declares the LORD. You fill in the part that says "Do not say, I am too _____."
Once you declare and decree that over your life God will do the rest!

+++

Date: Time:

Journal Entry:

Write the nugget you received from the Lord while completing the reading for today.

_____

_____

_____

_____

_____

_____

_____

Scripture Reading: Personal revelation today?

Prayer focus:

Day 20 ~ The P.R.I.C.E. of Destiny
~ Read 1 Corinthians 7
Scripture focus: 1 Corinthians 7:22-23

For the one who was a slave when called to faith in the Lord is the Lord's freed person; similarly, the one who was free when called is Christ's slave. You were bought at a price; do not become slaves of human beings.

~**W**hat is Destiny? Simply put, it is reaching and achieving the assignment God has placed on your life. It seems like this would be an easier task than it really is. Many times there are people and forces in this world to discourage us and they try to prevent many from reaching destiny. Other times we allow fear, finances and a lack of faith from reaching it. Once thing is for certain, once you make up in your mind that you are going to reach destiny, work towards it and achieve it, you understand that just like Jesus, we are going to pay a price.

- P – Persecution
- R – Rejection
- I – Isolation
- C – Cost you
- E – Everything

The Word states:

"As it is written, For thy sake we are killed all the day long; we are accounted as sheep for the slaughter." Romans 8:36

I want to know Christ and the power of his resurrection and the fellowship of sharing in his sufferings, becoming like him in his death, Philippians 3:10

Jesus suffered persecution, faced rejection, isolation and it cost Him everything. It's a price He was willing to pay for you and me. What more shall we face and do for Him?

Date: Time:

Journal Entry:

Write the nugget you received from the Lord while completing the reading for today.

_____

_____

_____

_____

_____

_____

_____

_____

_____

_____

_____

_____

Scripture Reading: Personal revelation today?

_____

_____

_____

_____

_____

_____

_____

_____

Prayer focus:

_____

_____

_____

_____

_____

~ Call on Him!
Some of the Names of God

ADONAI-JEHOVAH	The Lord is Sovereign	Genesis 12:2,8
ALPHA and OMEGA	The Beginning and the End	Revelation 1:8, 21:6, and 22:13
EL-ELYON	The most high God	Genesis 14:17-20, Isaiah 14:13-14
EL-SHADDAI	The God of the mountains or God Almighty	Genesis 17:1, Psalm 91:1
JEHOVAH-JIREH	The Lord will provide	Genesis 22:13-14
JEHOVAH-MACCADDESHEM	The Lord thy sanctifier	Exodus 31:13
JEHOVAH-RAPHA	The Lord our healer	Exodus 15:26
JEHOVAH-ROHI	The Lord my shepherd	Psalm 23:1
JEHOVAH-SHALOM	The Lord is peace	Judges 6:24
JEHOVAH-SHAMMAH	The Lord who is present	Ezekiel 48:35
JEHOVAH-TSIDKENU	The Lord our righteousness	Jeremiah 23:6
JEHOVAH—YAHWEH	God's divine salvation	Genesis 2:4

There are many more Names of God. Take some time to research them on your next date with Jesus!

Day 21 ~ The P.U.R.S.U.I.T of Destiny
~ Read 1 Samuel 30
Scripture focus: 1 Samuel 30:17-19

Then David attacked them from twilight until the evening of the next day. Not a man of them escaped, except four hundred young men who rode on camels and fled. So David recovered all that the Amalekites had carried away, and David rescued his two wives. And nothing of theirs was lacking, either small or great, sons or daughters, spoil or anything which they had taken from them; David recovered all.

~David's story of pursuing and recovering all is very inspirational. We know that David certainly understood and knew the P.R.I.C.E of destiny all to well. But here we also see that with the help of the Lord David knew how to pursue and recover all! What can we learn from David and how can we walk in victory while in the pursuit of recovering all?

- P – Perseverance
- U – Unrestricted Praise
- R – Risk Taker (must be a risk taker. Some things God will ask you to do will be outside of your comfort zone)
- S – Sacrifice (must be willing to offer a sacrifice and become a sacrifice for God)
- U – Unrestrained Worship
- I – Inquire of the Lord
- T – To Go (must be willing to go wherever, whenever and to whomever God sends)

Pursue and recover all now says the Lord!

+++

Date: Time:

Journal Entry:

Write the nugget you received from the Lord while completing the reading for today.

_____

_____

_____

_____

_____

_____

_____

_____

_____

_____

_____

_____

_____

Scripture Reading: Personal revelation today?

_____
_____
_____
_____
_____
_____
_____
_____
_____
_____

Prayer focus:

_____
_____
_____
_____

Day 22 ~ Do and Finish
~ Read: John 4
Scripture: John 4:31-35

In the meantime His disciples urged Him, saying, "Rabbi, eat." But He said to them, "I have food to eat of which you do not know." Therefore the disciples said to one another, "Has anyone brought Him anything to eat?" Jesus said to them, "My food is to do the will of Him who sent Me, and to finish His work. Do you not say, 'There are still four months and *then* comes the harvest'? Behold, I say to you, lift up your eyes and look at the fields, for they are already ripe for harvest.

~**W**hat a statement made by Jesus "My food is to do the will of Him who sent Me, and to finish His work..." What if we all had this mentality and thought process? I read this scripture and thought to myself how different our churches, ministries, and the world would be if the total focus was on doing the will and finishing the work. I remember a time when I was unemployed and needed a job desperately. God opened a door for me to work in the Non-Profit arena at a transitional housing facility. I loved the job and thanked God for employment. My job description basically consisted of finding housing for those entering or leaving the program. I wanted to do things routinely and quickly realized that this job was going to be anything but a routine assignment.

Many of the ladies had come from the most unimaginable circumstances. They were trying to survive and overcome the effects from drugs, alcohol, domestic violence situations, and homelessness. One day a young lady was distraught about life and was having difficulty processing how she found herself in this current situation. That day, and many more to follow, the Lord challenged me and let me know I was there to do His work along with my job. I was able to minister to this young lady and lead her to Christ. She went from preparing to commit suicide or homicide, to giving her life to Christ and getting baptized! Glory to God!

Those ladies helped me in ways they may never know. I ended up being laid off a few weeks later, but it was well, because I knew that I had done the will of the One who truly sent me, and I had finished the work assigned by God. God is challenging each one of us to Do His Will and Finish His Work!

Date:		Time:

Journal Entry:

Write the nugget you received from the Lord while completing the reading for today.

_____

_____

_____

_____

Scripture Reading: Personal revelation today?

Prayer focus:

Day 23 ~ The Battle is Not Yours!
~ Read: 2 Chronicles 20
Scripture focus: 2 Chronicles 20:15

The Lord says this to you: Be not afraid or dismayed at this great multitude; for the battle is not yours, but God's.

~"Thank you for choosing South Texas Radiology Imaging Centers for your mammography needs. As a federally accredited facility we are required to notify you of the results of your recent breast imaging evaluations. Your recent breast imaging exam showed an 'area of concern' that requires you to return for additional evaluation." Date: August 2010.

As I read those words, I had a thousand emotions, and a thousand thoughts to come rushing all at once. "An area of concern" - those four words grabbed me, held me, and didn't want to let me go. I had just turned 40 and I did what every woman is encouraged to do, get a mammogram. I went on a Tuesday for my routine annual doctor's appointment, got the mammogram, and thought no more of it. On Saturday this letter came in the mail, and I do not remember reading past "an area of concern."

I began to cry tears that didn't seem like they were my own and my very breath seemed to have left me. I called a few prayer warriors and I went to my church where I am the Pastor. I went, I cried, I lay out at the altar, and I prayed. I stayed for what seemed like hours, and just as I was getting up, I heard the Lord say "leave it at the altar." I thought to myself "that's what I was doing" and then He said it again "leave it at the altar." I took the letter and placed in under my pulpit at the altar. Then I heard him say, "No leave it all at the altar." I then placed the envelope that the letter had come in under the pulpit at the altar. I got up, left the church, and went home to prepare for Sunday Service.

I rescheduled my follow up appointment for the following Tuesday. Another mammogram followed by a sonogram and then more waiting to hear from the doctor. While I was waiting for the results, God said write this letter (journal entry) among other things. For the entire week I thought of all the things God had asked me to do. I thought of the things I did with no problem, the things that took courage, but mostly I thought about the things I hadn't done out of fear.

Cancer, death, and not living life to the fullest were on my mind. I wanted to see Niagara Falls, and reach the destiny God has spoken over my life. I am 40, single, employed for corporate America and a newly installed Pastor. I felt alone, lonely, and isolated as I began the mental "what if list." Then I heard the Lord say clearly "This battle is not yours." I had peace overtake me and I knew regardless of the results I was still in God's hands. I can truly say that I received a peace that really surpasses human understanding. A few days later I received a call from my doctor's office and a follow up letter which read; "the result of your mammogram and/or breast ultrasound imaging evaluation is NORMAL."

Was this a test of my Faith; Was this a test of Obedience; Was it the thing I needed to stop being comfortable, to face my fear of rejection, to get involved in something that I would not have been involved in, and have yet another Testimony; Or was it to make sure I truly live life to the fullest, write this book and pursue Destiny! I think the answer to all the above is a resounding Yes and Amen!

Date: Time:

Journal Entry:

Write the nugget you received from the Lord while completing the reading for today.

_____
_____
_____
_____
_____
_____
_____
_____
_____

Scripture Reading: Personal revelation today?

Prayer focus:

Day 24 ~ Just Stand
~ Read Ephesians 6
Scripture focus: Ephesians 6:10-13

Finally, be strong in the Lord and in his mighty power. Put on the full armor of God, so that you can take your stand against the devil's schemes. For our struggle is not against flesh and blood, but against the rulers, against the authorities, against the powers of this dark world and against the spiritual forces of evil in the heavenly realms. Therefore put on the full armor of God, so that when the day of evil comes, you may be able to stand your ground, and after you have done everything, to stand.

~**W**e live in a world where the news on the television, radio, or internet seems to get continually worse. There are times in our own lives when things seem to go down hill rapidly. What do you do when you have done all you know how do, and still do not have an answer? First, we have to understand and accept that many things are beyond our control. Death is going to occur, sickness will happen, a lost job or a financial crisis may come your way. When these things happen, they take us out of our normal everyday routine, and cause us to stop and take time to catch our breath.

We have to keep moving in our natural environments, but spiritually we have to stand. We have to know that we know, that we know, who God is, and who we are in the faith. When things come to shake and challenge our faith we have to dig deep and pray for God to give us the strength to survive the attack and stand our ground.

In order for this to happen and defeat the enemy, we have to pray and have the Word on the inside of us. Prayer is a lifestyle, not just something you do on Sunday, or when you are in crisis. Hiding the Word in your heart is not memorizing scripture, it is living the scriptures. It becomes who you are in every area of your life. It's who you are in the grocery store, the gym, the doctor's office, a family gathering, or on your job. You have to take a stand to always represent the Jesus on the inside of you. You can provide an encouraging word to others, but you can also encourage yourself, when all hell seems like it has broken out around you. The word says "Therefore put on the full armor of God, so that when the day of evil comes, you may be able to stand your ground, and after you have done everything, to stand." Trust God.

Date: Time:

Journal Entry:

Write the nugget you received from the Lord while completing the reading for today.

_____

_____

_____

Scripture Reading: Personal revelation today?

Prayer focus:

Day 25 ~ Take up Your Cross
~ Read Luke 9
Scripture focus: Luke 9:23-26

Then he said to them all: "Whoever wants to be my disciple must deny themselves and take up their cross daily and follow me. For whoever wants to save their life will lose it, but whoever loses their life for me will save it. What good is it for someone to gain the whole world, and yet lose or forfeit their very self? Whoever is ashamed of me and my words, the Son of Man will be ashamed of them when he comes in his glory and in the glory of the Father and of the holy angels.

~**M**y flesh must die. That's what I tell myself on a daily basis. I am a spiritual being living a human life, a human being living a spiritual life. I am spirit first and foremost. Taking up my cross and following Christ means at the end of the day _____ has to die to self as it has to be God's way or no way. Not my will, but God's will. Of course this is easier said than done when we live in such a "me and what I want I get and will do what ever it takes to get there" world.

I remember one job years ago in corporate America, where getting to the top was the focus and primary goal. People did all sorts of things to get the attention of the man or woman in charge. I had people use me, slander my name and so forth on a constant basis. I had a choice to make: retaliate, leave, or wait on God for my promotion. My flesh wanted to get back at all these people, but once you are truly sold out to and for this Gospel, you understand whose you are and who you are in Him. God allowed me to stay on that job long enough to get the promotions that can only come from Him, and put me in a position to be able to tell people about the real "Man" in charge on a daily basis. By the time I left, most of those same people had left he company, and the ones who had gotten promoted from their ruthlessness were miserable. God allowed me to leave happy and walking with the full authority that comes with following Christ.

We must be a people who are Kingdom minded; meaning every thought, action and deed must be to benefit the Kingdom of God. God knows what is best for us. When we allow Him total access to every area of our lives; when we truly serve others more than ourselves; when we not only accept Jesus Christ as our personal Savior but also allow Him to be Lord over our lives; then we can say we have taken up our cross and are following Christ. Jesus left heaven to come to earth for us, the least we can do is leave our selfishness and follow Him to one day leave this earth and make Heaven our home.

Date: Time:

Journal Entry:

Write the nugget you received from the Lord while completing the reading for today.

Scripture Reading: Personal revelation today?

Prayer focus:

Day 26 ~ Task Master
~ Read: Nehemiah 4
Scripture focus: Nehemiah 4:6

So we built the wall, and the entire wall was joined together up to half its height, for the people had a mind to work.

~Distraction, delay and discouragement are a few of the words to describe what happens when we have become overwhelmed with life. We all have one thousand and one roles to fill, and several hats to wear. Many times they all take on a life of their own. Along the way we also are given assignments by God to complete. I have found that when you finally make up your mind to serve Him completely and begin to complete the task that He has assigned, distraction, delay, and discouragement become tools used to prevent us from moving forward.

Distraction and discouragement may show up in the form of a sickness, extreme fatigue, inability to move on from a painful experience, a person or persons, and increased pressures and demands that show up all of a sudden, just to name a few. Typically, once we are distracted we then begin to delay or put off the things on the spiritual hit list God has given us. We begin to put it off until we feel better, until the child feels better, until you get more sleep, until your job isn't as busy, until uncle Bob gets his act together, and so on and so on. Many of us do this and before we realize it - days, months and years have passed us by and we still have not completed a single task. I am sure you know of people who went to the grave with a long list of dreams, visions and task that were never completed, nor fulfilled due to a lifetime of distractions and constant delays.

Do not become one of those people! The believer has to choose to operate on a different level, while understanding that these things are designed to keep you from fulfilling the will of God. I want you to highlight, underline, or write down the next sentence to get you past distraction and delay. Each time you find yourself being distracted or delayed read it out loud! <u>I have a task from the Master and only the Master can help me complete my task</u>! God gave the task, He is the Master planner, and He alone will help you complete the task.

Date: Time:

Journal Entry:

Write the nugget you received from the Lord while completing the reading for today.

_____

_____

_____

_____

_____

Scripture Reading: Personal revelation today?

Prayer focus:

Day 27 ~ More Power
~ Read: 2 Corinthians 12
Scripture: 2 Corinthians 12:9-10

My grace is sufficient for you, for My strength is made perfect in weakness. Therefore most gladly I will rather boast in my infirmities, that the power of Christ may rest upon me. Therefore I take pleasure in infirmities, in reproaches, in needs, in persecutions, in distresses, for Christ's sake. For when I am weak, then I am strong.

~**Do** you know what date rape is? It is defined as an assault or attempted assault usually committed by a new acquaintance involving sexual intercourse without mutual consent. Until the age of twenty one I had no concept of it either. I had met a guy, who worked in the law enforcement field, through a friend. I met him on a Thursday, we talked and he asked me if I could cook and it led to an invitation for dinner in a week or so. We spoke on the phone the following day and he asked if he could stop by because he was in the neighborhood and just wanted to see me. He came over and in less than thirty minutes I was attacked and raped. He said the normal things, we knew each other, and I really wanted it, although I was screaming no and stop at the top of my lungs.

When he left I called a friend who told me to forget about it because he worked in the law enforcement field. I never called the police because I thought who would believe me. Years later, I realized, I blamed myself for an incident that was not my fault. During my many, many, weak and utterly helpless moments, I have asked God why? Sometimes I get an answer, but many times like you, I do not get one. It's during these times that we must lean on the Word and our faith. When I am weak, God is indeed strong. When I have no strength, I know that His strength is made perfect in my weakness. The more I have gone through, the more power God gives me. The greater the calling is on your life, the greater the warfare is in your life. God has given you more power; use it to help someone else.

Date: Time:

Journal Entry:

Write the nugget you received from the Lord while completing the reading for today.

_____

_____

_____

_____

_____

_____

_____

Scripture Reading: Personal revelation today?

Prayer focus:

Day 28 ~ Never Satisfied
~ Read Acts 2
Scripture focus: Acts 2:2-4

And suddenly there came a sound from heaven as of a rushing mighty wind, and it filled the entire house where they were sitting. And there appeared unto them cloven tongues like as of fire, and it sat upon each of them. And they were all filled with the Holy Ghost, and began to speak with other tongues, as the Spirit gave them utterance.

~**W**hen was the last time you had a truly awesome, amazing, encounter with the Holy Ghost? The scripture for today is one of my favorite scriptures in the Bible. I cannot imagine life without the Holy Spirit. So many times we go to church Sunday after Sunday, but we get use to the service to the point where we are not in expectation when we walk through the door. We should earnestly seek a new encounter with the Father, Son and Holy Ghost every single day of our lives! I have begun to make this request and I am always amazed at when and how God shows up.

There are times when I am reading the Word or in prayer and feel His presence so strong. Other times I am in church or in fellowship with other believers. The times that amaze me the most come when I am in my bathroom, or my kitchen, or my car, and the Holy Spirit overtakes me and the tears begin to fall. I cry and wave my hand, or kneel. I have an encounter with the Master and He has let me know how much he loves me, how much I mean to him, and how much He loves my worship. During the times that I have mountain top encounters, I do not want to come down. I want to stay there and never leave. I have found that these encounters create a hunger inside of me that is never satisfied. I wait in eager anticipation of my next encounter with Him in the secret place. I want to be in the Holy of Holies! The higher He takes me, the more I want. The more I love Him; I want to love Him more. The more I worship; the more I need of Him!

My prayer is that as you are reading and writing for these 40 days, and as you are having your dates with Jesus, you are at the place of asking and receiving new encounters that make you say to yourself - "I am never satisfied."

Date: Time:

Journal Entry:

Write the nugget you received from the Lord while completing the reading for today.

_____

_____

_____

_____

_____

Scripture Reading: Personal revelation today?

Prayer focus:

Day 29 ~ Heal My Finances!
~ Read: Isaiah 58
Scripture focus: Isaiah 58:8

Then your light will break forth like the dawn, and your healing will quickly appear; then your righteousness will go before you, and the glory of the LORD will be your rear guard.

~**A** life long friend asked me to pray for God to heal her from Sickle Cell Anemia, or at least the associated pain. As you may know this is a serious disease in which the body makes sickle-shaped red blood cells. "Sickle-shaped" means that the red blood cells are shaped like a "C." The clumps of sickle cells block blood flow in the blood vessels that lead to the limbs and organs. Blocked blood vessels can cause pain, serious infections, and organ damage. I began to pray for her healing, but not just for her sickle cell, but for healing physically, mentally, and emotionally. A year passed and I continued to pray. She called me one day and said "for the first time in my life I am pain free today." A few months later we spoke again and she called to tell me her marriage was being healed. A few months later she reported more things in her life that were being healed; things and areas of her life that she did not even realize need healing!

I know that you're asking what in the world does this have to do with finances. We can also pray for God to heal our finances. Keep in mind this will mean healing you! This does not mean you are going to be debt free over night, or that your credit report will miraculously be wiped clean. So again, I know you are asking "how can God help me heal my finances?"

- He may have to heal you mentally by changing your spending habits.
- He may have to heal your pre-conceived thoughts by making you more conscious to use cash or your debit card instead of the plastic.
- He may have to heal you by allowing you to recognize what triggers you to go on a spending spree and then dealing with the issue at hand.
- He may have to heal you emotionally by identifying the root cause of your poor financial choices.
- He will help you establish a plan in order for you not to repeat the same mistakes.
- He may have to heal you spiritually for you to realize He and He alone is your source and will fill every need.

My friend still has sickle cell but spends less time in the hospital or in pain. She wanted prayer to heal in one area but God desired that she be healed in every other area, which has caused her overall health to improve. You are praying for God to heal your finances by giving you more money and God desires to heal you in every area concerning your finances by giving you more of Him!

Date: Time:

Journal Entry:

Write the nugget you received from the Lord while completing the reading for today.

Scripture Reading: Personal revelation today?

Prayer focus:

Day 30 ~ Wrap Me in Your Arms
~ Read: Colossians 3
Scripture focus: Colossians 3:1-4

Since, then, you have been raised with Christ, set your hearts on things above, where Christ is, seated at the right hand of God. Set your minds on things above, not on earthly things. For you died, and your life is now hidden with Christ in God. When Christ, who is your life, appears, then you also will appear with him in glory.

~**T**here is nothing like a warm hug to say hello or I love you. Hugs are intimate gestures that require us to open our arms and embrace another human being. Likewise, God opens his arms and invites us into his presence and as the scripture for today states "and your life is now hidden with Christ in God." In His presence we will find:

Anointing	Authority
Blessings	Boldness
Comfort	Correction
Courage	Deliverance
Discipline	Encouragement
Endurance	Faith
Favor	Forgiveness
Freedom	Grace
Guidance	Healing
Hope	Inspiration
Joy	Justice
Kindness	Love
Mercy	Motivation
Newness	Obedience
Patience	Peace

Power	Provision
Protection	Revelation
Restoration	Righteousness
Safety	Salvation
Strength	Trust
Truth	Victory
Wisdom	Wonders

As you write your journal entry today write some additional words to describe what you feel in the presence of the Lord!

Date: Time:

Journal Entry:

Write the nugget you received from the Lord while completing the reading for today.

_____

_____

_____

_____

_____

_____

_____

Scripture Reading: Personal revelation today?

Prayer focus:

~Words of Encouragement

~I am sure you have noticed by now that I share many personal testimonies throughout this devotional. God has called me to share my story and my testimonies with the world in order to help someone else. I want you to know that I survived and so can you. God gave me the following daily confession while writing this book:

Father, today I give you thanks and praise. I thank you for keeping me through the night. I thank you for traveling mercy. Most of all I thank you for the free gift of salvation that came through your son Jesus Christ. Praise the Lord. Praise God in his sanctuary; praise Him in his mighty heavens. Let everything that has breath praise the Lord.

Father, forgive me for anything I have said, done, or thought that was not in line with You or your Word. Father, forgive me for anything I have said, done, or thought against another human being, including any destructive behaviors against myself. Father, forgive our debts as we forgive our debtors.

Father, I declare that this day I commit to believe your Word that I am the head and not the tail; I am above and not beneath; I am the lender and not the borrower, I declare that I am fearfully and wonderfully made. I am focused, faithful and walking in the favor of the Lord!

Father, I declare that this day I commit to be about my Father's business. I must be about my father's business in my service, my fasting, my walk, my talk, my prayer, my praise, my worship and my love! Hallelujah!

Salvation and Glory and Power belong to our God! Amen, Amen and Amen!

Day 31 ~ Everything I Need
~ Read: Philippians 4
Scripture focus: Philippians 4:11-13

Not that I speak in regard to need, for I have learned in whatever state I am, to be content: I know how to be abased, and I know how to abound. Everywhere and in all things I have learned both to be full and to be hungry, both to abound and to suffer need. I can do all things through Christ who strengthens me.

~Life has a way of being very unpredictable. Life often reminds me of the four seasons, and the weather that sometimes accompanies them. We have winter, spring, summer and fall. Each has its own distinct weather patterns but every now and then we get some unpredictable weather sequences. We do not get to pick if it is a bad winter storm or an extreme heat wave; we just have to have patience, endurance and be able to survive it. Just like life, if it is the unexpected death of a loved one, a failed marriage, financial ruin, natural disasters or a spiritual crisis, it is during these difficult times that our faith and patience are truly tested. Demonstrating faith and patience during these times demonstrate a trust in God that is just indescribable.

I have found out how important faith and patience are in my life, and how they work together. I have experienced violent and unexpected storms in my life that resulted in loss, after loss, after loss. I initially was so devastated and angry that faith and patience were the last things on my mind. In all honesty, after the shock wore off, I immediately started questioning God. I was angry with God. I found it difficult to go to church and receive the word as it was going forth. It was even more difficult to read the Bible, or pray without constant distractions in my mind. At this time my faith felt weak and my patience felt non-existent. God being God did only what He can do. He provided a way of escape for me. I received a phone call from my brother who heard the despair in my voice and God used him to speak this following statement: "The only one you can depend on in this life is God. He will never leave you nor forsake you. His promises are true, you have to walk in faith and have patience. You must trust God totally." It was like my spirit just opened up and received every morsel as if it was my last meal. It was then that I realized that God has everything I need!

I know that I can do all things through Christ who strengthens me. I know that just like the weather and seasons, I too am going to go through seasons, but God has promised me full and total restoration in every area of my life. How do I know - because God kept me when I couldn't keep myself!

Date: Time:

Journal Entry:

Write the nugget you received from the Lord while completing the reading for today.

_____

_____

Scripture Reading: Personal revelation today?

Prayer focus:

Day 32 ~ Be Still
~ Read: Psalm 46
Scripture: Psalm 46:10

Be still, and know that I *am* God.

~**T**his scripture is simple, yet it is packed with wisdom, knowledge and power. When was the last time you had to make a difficult decision? When you made the decision was it based on your emotional condition or your spiritual condition? Recently, I experienced a mini crisis and had to make some choices that would impact the next direction for my life. I spent much time in prayer, but I had been very emotional as well, and I wanted to make sure I was hearing from God. I sought the opinion of several family members and a few friends. My mother stated "You need to go somewhere by yourself and be still before the Lord. You need to quiet your emotions and wait until He answers." In other words it was time for a date with Jesus.

I decided to go for a drive and ended up at the beach. I walked along the beach watching the people, the birds, and the waves. As the waves came ashore I heard that still small voice saying "Be still and know that I am God." Just then the very elements of my surroundings became my inspiration.

- **The Sand** – The sand had footprints and tire tracks, but no two were the same. Likewise, my path in this life is unique and was designed just for me. My path was one that was chosen before the foundation of the earth. I understood more than ever that not everyone would approve nor agree, but it did not, and does not matter. God has a plan for my life and I will only reach destiny through obedience and following God.

- **The Birds** – The birds were all in various stages of being a bird. Some were flying; some were in the water; while others were on dry ground. No matter where they were God was providing for them. Something on the inside of them gave them direction and natural protection. God had and will continue to do the same thing for me.

- **The Water** – The waves came ashore one after another. No human force could make them neither come ashore nor stop them. They were destined to crash and go back out to sea. No matter how big or small the storm, God is in control. Just then I thought how God spoke to the winds and the waves saying "Peace be still."

I received the answer to my dilemma before leaving the beach. I also knew that going forward; I would not make any decisions while under any kind of stress. Family and friends mean well, but God knows my future. No matter what you are facing today please be still and wait on God. He knows what's best for you.

Date: Time:

Journal Entry:

Write the nugget you received from the Lord while completing the reading for today.

_____

_____

_____

_____

_____

_____

_____

_____

_____

_____

_____

_____

_____

_____

Scripture Reading: Personal revelation today?

_____

_____

_____

_____

_____

_____

_____

_____

Prayer focus:

_____

_____

_____

_____

_____

_____

Day 33 ~ Use Your Tool Belt
~ Read: Psalm 119
Scripture: Psalm 119:10-16

With my whole heart I have sought You; Oh, let me not wander from Your commandments! Your word I have hidden in my heart, That I might not sin against You. Blessed *are* You, O LORD! Teach me Your statutes. With my lips I have declared All the judgments of Your mouth. I have rejoiced in the way of Your testimonies, As much *as* in all riches. I will meditate on Your precepts, And contemplate Your ways. I will delight myself in Your statutes; I will not forget Your word.

~**T**here is something about visiting the big hardware superstores. The isles are filled with everything you need for your home. You can build something from scratch, you can buy items to finish a project, and they have several tools to use regardless of how big or small the project. They also have helpful associates ready and willing to help you if you do not know where an item is located or how to use it.

In the same way God has provided us with several tools to help us in our homes, on our jobs, in church, or when we are all by ourselves. What are these tools you may be asking? First, we have the Holy Bible. Every need and every answer you are searching for can be found right in the Word. It is called the "Good Book" for a reason. "Your word I have hidden in my heart, that I might not sin against You...I will not forget Your word."

Secondly, we have the tool of prayer. "With my lips I have declared All the judgments of Your mouth." Prayer is our way of being able to have two way communications with God. Never underestimate the power of prayer. Thirdly, we have the tool of praise and worship! God created us to fellowship with Him and God delights in our praise, our adoration and our worship. "Blessed *are* You, O LORD!... I have rejoiced in the way of Your testimonies, As *much as* in all riches. I will meditate on Your precepts, And contemplate Your ways."

God sent one of the final tools to us in the person of the Holy Spirit. The Holy Spirit is our helper, our built in warning system, and our guide to lead us and direct us. God did not leave you, he will never leave you. He also left us tools to use to navigate this thing called life.

Date: Time:

Journal Entry:

Write the nugget you received from the Lord while completing the reading for today.

_____

_____

_____

_____

Scripture Reading: Personal revelation today?

Prayer focus:

**Day 34 ~ Scales Falling from Your Eyes
~ Read: Acts 9
Scripture: Acts 9:16-18**

"For I will show him how many things he must suffer for My name's sake." And Ananias went his way and entered the house; and laying his hands on him he said, "Brother Saul, the Lord Jesus, who appeared to you on the road as you came, has sent me that you may receive your sight and be filled with the Holy Spirit." Immediately there fell from his eyes *something* like scales, and he received his sight at once; and he arose and was baptized.

~**D**o you remember the day the scales fell off your eyes, the day when you noticed the butterflies and appreciated the rain? Do you remember the day the scales fell off your eyes, and the day you cried tears of pure joy because you made the most important decision of your life, or had the most amazing revelation of your life? For some, it's the day they gave their life to Christ, and for others it's the day you really understood who He was and is in your life.

I grew up in church and officially gave my life to Christ at the age of twelve. I was baptized and continued to go to church. However, the scales of recognition didn't fall off my eyes until I was 18 years old. I went to church one Sunday after hanging out all night with friends. I was tired and if I tell the truth I didn't want to go that Sunday. My Pastor at that time had been my Pastor for four or five years. The title of his sermon that Sunday was "It's Personal." He spoke concerning a personal relationship with

Jesus and how we couldn't have this relationship through someone else. We couldn't have it through our father, mother, sister, brother, or even the Pastor himself. Now I am sure he said this before, but this particular Sunday I heard it, received it in my heart, mind, and spirit in a whole new way. The scales fell from my eyes. I was on yet another Date with Him! I am so glad I kept my Divine appointment in spite of my flesh.

I pray as you are reading this, writing journal entries, and praying each day that God is removing the scales from your eyes. Things that previously made you blind are being removed. Receive your sight, receive your sight again!

Date: Time:

Journal Entry:

Write the nugget you received from the Lord while completing the reading for today.

_____

_____

_____

_____

_____

Scripture Reading: Personal revelation today?

Prayer focus:

Day 35 ~ Spiritual Urgency
~ Read: Genesis 32
Scripture: Genesis 32:24-26

Then Jacob was left alone; and a Man wrestled with him until the breaking of day. Now when He saw that He did not prevail against him, He touched the socket of his hip; and the socket of Jacob's hip was out of joint as He wrestled with him. And He said, "Let Me go, for the day breaks." But he said, "I will not let You go unless You bless me!"

~Someone please call 911! How many days have you felt like God had left you, forgotten you, or forsaken you? Those times are some of the worst times in the life of a believer. You feel like all hell has broken loose and you are the only one who is going through this current crisis or situation. You have tried to talk to your spouse, your friends, your co-workers, and even your prayer partners, but no one seems to get it. You find yourself restless and waking up at all hours of the night. You are irritable, moody, and do not want to be bothered. You cry, pray, and desperately search for a resolution. Then one day you just get so frustrated you tell God "wait, I am not going to move unless you bless me, unless I get an answer, unless!"

There are many situations and issues in our lives that will not be dealt with until we fall on our knees or on our faces and call out to the Father. He is the original ICE (In Case of Emergency) 911 emergency systems. He is our GPS (Global Positioning System) when we are lost and our Doppler radar in the midst of our storms. He is the original Peace maker, Joy restorer and Hope filler! Call on Him, you will never get a busy signal or a message stamped return to sender!

Date: Time:

Journal Entry:

Write the nugget you received from the Lord while completing the reading for today.

_____

_____

_____

_____

_____

_____

_____

_____

_____

_____

Scripture Reading: Personal revelation today?

Prayer focus:

Day 36 ~ My Tears, Your Tears
~ Read: Psalm 30
Scripture: Psalm 30:4-5

Sing praise to the LORD, you saints of His, And give thanks at the remembrance of His holy name. For His anger *is but for* a moment, His favor *is for* life; Weeping may endure for a night, But joy *comes* in the morning.

~**M**y father was a good man who lived his life trying to beat his addictions to drugs and alcohol. Despite his addictions, he was my father, and my daddy. I loved him and always believed in him and vice versa. He was a professional cook and had many gifts and talents. He never got to use most of his gifts - as one hit; one needle in his arm, changed his life forever. I spent many days in my young years watching my father destroy himself slowly but surely. He went to countless rehabilitation centers and hospitals through the years. There were many days when he would overdose and find himself in the hospital again. The last time he took an overdose, I was the one who found him.

My father never fully recovered and lost the battle of addiction and also his life. When he died I didn't cry or react. I was numb and kept going on with the daily activities of life. Five years later I had another tragic event in my life and when I cried, I cried for what seemed like an eternity. I had never went through the grieving process years earlier and now it all came rushing in like a tidal wave.

We know that our tears have a few purposes in the human body. One of which is a physical release from our emotional pain. Now please understand, we cry and then there are times when we weep. I wept that year for all the losses I had experienced. I wept, and wept, and couldn't stop those tears. It was as if they had a mind of their own. It was cleansing and therapeutic all at the same time. In the midst of those tears I began praising and worshipping God. I went through a process and over time I began to gain my joy back. No matter what circumstance you are facing today I want you to know that God is a healer and our ultimate comforter. Go ahead - cry, weep, and go through your process. But most assuredly I tell you "Weeping may endure for a night, but joy *comes* in the morning."

"Jesus wept." John 11:35

Date: Time:

Journal Entry:

Write the nugget you received from the Lord while completing the reading for today.

_____

_____

_____

Scripture Reading: Personal revelation today?

Prayer focus:

Day 37 ~ I Hear the Sound of Rain
~ Read: 1 Kings 18
Scripture: 1 Kings 18:41-44a

Then Elijah said to Ahab, "Go up, eat and drink; for *there is* the sound of abundance of rain." So Ahab went up to eat and drink. And Elijah went up to the top of Carmel; then he bowed down on the ground, and put his face between his knees, and said to his servant, "Go up now, look toward the sea." So he went up and looked, and said, "*There is* nothing." And seven times he said, "Go again." Then it came to pass the seventh *time,* that he said, "There is a cloud, as small as a man's hand, rising out of the sea!"

~Famine, drought, or even a recession can cause people to rely on a source other than them. We live in a world where we have an abundance of money, water, and food but we still witness homelessness, poverty, world hunger, and so much more. I live in Texas which is a state with historically low rain fall totals. Recently, each morning when I awoke I had begun to hear the sound of rain. I would look out my window and it would be dry outside. This went on for weeks at a time. I began to ask God for the significance of my experience. He led me to this scripture and then through reading the Word I began to gain understanding.

Even in the driest place of our lives God can send the rain. When all others have given up on the God we serve, He will surely come through. The rain can come in the form of comfort, peace, or tangible provisions. We must wait in eager expectation. We must also understand that when the rain comes it is not just for us, but also for somebody else. God will send abundance or an overflow and our sincere responsibility is to then help someone else. You and I can then be used as someone else's sound of rain - with one meal, one kind word, or one act of kindness extended to another human being.

Date: Time:

Journal Entry:

Write the nugget you received from the Lord while completing the reading for today.

_____

_____

_____

_____

_____

_____

_____

_____

Scripture Reading: Personal revelation today?

Prayer focus:

Day 38 ~ Increase In Faith and Patience
~ Read: Hebrews 11
Scripture: Hebrews 11:1-3

Now faith is the substance of things hoped for, the evidence of things not seen. For by it the elders obtained a *good* testimony. By faith we understand that the worlds were framed by the word of God, so that the things which are seen were not made of things which are visible.

~**A**s you have read this devotional you have read many of my testimonies. I am one who is no longer afraid to tell the truth about my life. I am a very transparent person and I know that God will use my story to help someone else, and He will get the Glory. I can now tell others the true meaning of faith and patience because of my personal walk and many testimonies. There are several passages of scripture in the Bible regarding faith and patience. Today's reading focus concentrated on faith. I will list a few scriptures here that focus on patience. These are the ones that continue to help me stand.

- Romans 5:3-4 "And not only that but we also glory in tribulations, knowing that tribulations produces perseverance; and perseverance, character; and character hope."
- 2 Corinthians 6:4 "But in all things we commend ourselves as ministers of God: in much patience, in tribulations, in needs, in distress."
- 1 Timothy 6:11-12 "But you, man of God, flee from all this, and pursue righteousness, godliness, faith, love, endurance and gentleness. Fight the good fight of the faith. Take hold of the eternal

life to which you were called when you made your good confession in the presence of many witnesses."
- Hebrews 6:12 and 15 "That you do not become sluggish, but imitate those who through faith and patience inherit the promises." And "so after he had patiently endured he obtained the promise."
- Hebrews 12:1-2 "Therefore we also, since we are surrounded by so great a cloud of witnesses, let us lay aside every weight, and the sin which so easily ensnares us and let us run with perseverance the race that is set before us. Looking unto Jesus, the author and finisher of our faith, who for the joy that was set before Him endured the cross, despising the shame, and has sat down at the right hand of the throne of God."

Date: Time:

Journal Entry:

Write the nugget you received from the Lord while completing the reading for today.

_____

_____

_____

_____

Scripture Reading: Personal revelation today?

Prayer focus:

Day 39 ~ Trust God
~ Read: Nahum 1
Scripture: Nahum 1:7

The LORD is good, a refuge in times of trouble. He cares for those who trust in him.

~Have you ever had difficulty trusting God? Many people will respond with an overwhelming yes. What does it mean to trust? The word trust is defined as reliance on the integrity, strength, ability, surety, etc., of a person or thing; confidence. It seems that we are able to trust many things in this life. We can trust a driver to get us to our destination, a pilot to fly and land safely, a chair to hold when we sit down, a pay check to be in the bank, a spouse to be faithful and the list goes on.

I remember when I moved from Georgia to Texas and I used a moving company for the first time in my life. I trusted that the moving company would deliver my items in a safe and timely manner. I had several delays in the process, and began to wonder if I had done the right thing, and if I had chosen the right company. I began to doubt and worry. Then a truth hit me that there was nothing I could do about it but wait, hope, and trust God. Like so many other times in my life I believe Jesus was looking to see how I was going to go through this process. Was I going to complain, get agitated and upset, or was I going to totally trust Him?

We seem to be able to trust everything and everyone else with greater ease than we trust God. When it comes to God we tend to wonder, doubt, and question.

Many of you are facing various situations in your life right now, which you simply cannot do anything about, and other things that are beyond your control. Regardless of the situation you are facing today, God wants you to trust Him.

Jesus trusted the Father to send Him from Heaven to earth, to the cross, to the grave, and back to Heaven. Surely you and I can trust God today and through all of our tomorrows!

Date: Time:

Journal Entry:

Write the nugget you received from the Lord while completing the reading for today.

_____

_____

_____

_____

_____

_____

_____

Scripture Reading: Personal revelation today?

Prayer focus:

Day 40 ~ 40 Days and 40 Nights
~ Read: Matthew 4
Scripture: Matthew 4:1-4

Then Jesus was led up by the Spirit into the wilderness to be tempted by the devil. And when He had fasted forty days and forty nights, afterward He was hungry. Now when the tempter came to Him, he said, "If You are the Son of God, command that these stones become bread." But He answered and said, "It is written, 'Man shall not live by bread alone, but by every word that proceeds from the mouth of God."

~There is a true Biblical significance to the number forty. Let's take a look at a few:
- Moses stayed with the Lord for 40 days and 40 nights, without eating any food or drinking any water. [Exodus 34:28]
- Spies searched out the land of Canaan for 40 days. [Num 13:25]
- Noah waited another 40 days after it rained before he opened a window in the Ark. [Gen 8:6]
- Elijah walked 40 days and 40 nights to the mountain of the Lord, Mount Horeb. [1Kings 19:8]
- It rained for 40 days and 40 nights when God wanted to cleanse the world and start over. [*Genesis 7:12*]
- The Israelites spent 40 years in the wilderness. This was one year for each day they explored the Promised Land. [*Exodus 16:35*]
- Jesus fasted for 40 days in the wilderness. [Matthew 3:17]

- Jesus was seen in the earth 40 days after His crucifixion. [Acts 1:3 NIV]

Today is the 40th day for this devotional but it is not the end of your dates with Jesus. It has taken me approximately thirty six days to write this entire book. I had many days where it flowed and others when I had to wait to hear what the Lord wanted me to say. I started this during a twenty one day fast which I completed successfully. I am encouraging you to begin a task that God has assigned and set a timeline to complete it. Challenge yourself to complete something specific every 40 days and begin to walk in purpose! Have continual communion with God and continue to keep a journal. It is encouraging and rewarding to read a previous journal entry and see how the Lord answered your prayer or how He spoke to you on a particular day.

Make a choice not to just live and exist. Everything that happened to you has made you stronger and wiser. Trust God with every fiber of your life!

Date: Time:

Journal Entry:

Write the nugget you received from the Lord while completing the reading for today.

Scripture Reading: Personal revelation today?

Prayer focus:

~ Conclusion

According to 2 Timothy 3:16-17 it states that all Scripture is God breathed and is useful for teaching, rebuking, correcting, and training in righteousness so that the man of God may be complete, thoroughly equipped for every good work. Therefore, the Word of God in the life of a Christian is the road map. It literally is a compass for our journey on earth. The Word in the form of the Bible also represents direction and divine protection.

Once someone has given his or her life to Christ, then the true journey begins. The first question most of us have is what now? Christians need and want direction. We receive it from out leaders, through fellowship, through prayer, and primarily from the Word of God. How to live and walk this Christian journey is outlined for us in the Word. Every true leader or fellow Christian gets direction from the Word in order to be able to direct someone else.

As with any journey we sometimes get lost, go astray, stumble and fall, but thanks be to God, we then experience God's correction and protection. God's Word provides discipline in an undisciplined world. When the Word corrects us, we must be willing to repent, ask for forgiveness, and be willing to endure the correction or judgment that God allows. We have to understand that persecutions will come. 2 Timothy 3:12 states "...all who desire to live godly in Christ Jesus will suffer persecution" - it is then that we have to know, that we know, we are covered by God's divine protection.

All Christians need to know the Word of God for themselves because vs. 13 states "but evil men and impostors will grow worse, deceiving and being deceived." When you know the Word, when life happens, when you hear an unsound doctrine, you will know the truth for yourself. Knowing the Word is not quoting it verbatim; it is living it, and hiding the word in your heart.

Our Final Date with Jesus, of course, will take place when He returns. "Look, he is coming with the clouds," and "every eye will see him, even those who pierced him"; and all peoples on earth "will mourn because of him." So shall it be! Amen. "I am the Alpha and the Omega," says the Lord God, "who is, and who was, and who is to come, the Almighty." Revelation 1:7-8

I pray that this devotional-Bible Study-journal has encouraged you, motivated you, challenged you, healed and restored you, for the journey ahead.

Always In His Service...

~ **Additional Journal entry pages:**

About the Author:

Awesome, Prolific, Profound, Energizing and Motivational are just some the mere words that have been used to describe this Woman of God! She enjoys serving God and sharing her testimony with all who will listen. She has survived insurmountable odds and now desires to set the atmosphere for freedom in worship while speaking deliverance into the lives of God's people. She has hosted retreats, conferences and even held church online! Tammy has also been featured on television, radio, newspaper and in Charisma's SpiritLed Woman Magazine's June/July 2007 issue. She travels and ministers at conferences, retreats and many other venues. In 2011 she held the first Healing Hurting Women Everywhere Conference where many were healed, set free and delivered.

Tammy is a dedicated mother, works in corporate America as a Credit Counselor and Social Media Specialist. She is also the founder of Free Worship Deliverance Ministries. She is currently working on her second book, a Bible study and a mentoring program.

Contact the author:

www.prophettammybradford.com

www.freeworshipdeliveranceministries.com

Email: pastortammy3@att.net

Find us on Facebook: prophettammybradford

Twitter: @pastortammyb

Made in the USA
Middletown, DE
26 June 2017